Spencer, ♡

The beginning
of your own herb
garden perhaps - recipes, too
which I know you enjoy ☺

Love, hugs & kisses,
Pegs

Christ...

THE HERB BASKET

# Marjoram

## Mint &
## Marigold

THE HERB BASKET

# Marjoram

## Mint &
## Marigold

PHOTOGRAPHY BY GLORIA NICOL

*Text by Hazel Evans*

JG
PRESS

Origanum majorana · Mentha spicata · Calendula officinalis · Mentha spicata · Calendula officinalis · Origanum majorana · Mentha spicata · Calendula officinalis · Origanum majorana · Mentha spicata · Calendula officinalis · Origanum majorana · Calendula officinalis · Mentha spicata · Origanum majorana

THE HERB BASKET
*Marjoram, Mint, and Marigold*

*Designed and created by*
THE BRIDGEWATER BOOK COMPANY LTD.

*Written by Hazel Evans*
*Photography by Gloria Nicol*

*Designer: Jane Lanaway*
*Project editors: Veronica Sperling/Christine McFadden*
*Page makeup: Chris Lanaway*
*Step illustrations: Vana Haggerty*
*Border illustration: Pauline Allen*
*Cover: Annie Moss*
*American adaptation: Josephine Bacon*

CLB 4498
© 1996 COLOUR LIBRARY BOOKS LTD
Published in the USA 1996 by JG Press
Distributed by World Publications, Inc.

The JG Press imprint is a trademark of
JG Press, Inc., 455 Somerset Avenue,
North Dighton, MA 02764

Color separation by Tien Wah Press
Printed and bound in Singapore by Tien Wah Press

ISBN 1-57215-109-9

# CONTENTS

| | | | | |
|---|---|---|---|---|
| The Joy of Herbs | 10 | | Barbecues | 34 |
| Introducing Marjoram | 13 | | Casseroles | 37 |
| Introducing Mint | 16 | | Herb Cheeses | 38 |
| Introducing Marigold | 19 | | Marigold Cakes | 40 |
| Plant Care | 20 | | Mint Candies | 42 |
| Harvesting | 22 | | Drinks with Mint | 44 |
| Drying your Herbs | 25 | | Mint Chutney and Raita | 47 |
| A Herbal Rock Garden | 26 | | Painted Herb Pots | 48 |
| A Kitchen Planter | 27 | | Two Potpourris | 50 |
| Cut Herbs for Decoration | 29 | | Creams and Fresheners | 52 |
| A Herb hanging Basket | 29 | | Conditioners and Rinses | 54 |
| Herb Salads | 30 | | Wash Balls and Soap | 56 |
| Mixed Herb Bread | 32 | | Kitchen Sachets | 58 |
| Marigold Bread Rolls | 33 | | Index | 60 |

# THE JOY OF HERBS

*Marjoram*                    *Mint*                    *Marigold*

n herb, says the dictionary, is "a plant of which leaves, flower, and stem are used for food, medicine, scent, and flavor." They are also entwined in history.

The first books in the world were written about herbs and herbals, and they are certainly some of the most beautiful books that have been handed down to us. As far as we know, the first person to compose a herbal was the Chinese Emperor Chin Nong in 2700 BC, but there may have been others before him. Herbal lore was also inscribed on ancient Assyrian tablets, while Greek herbals listed some 500 plants, all of which we cultivate today. But it was Discorides, in the first century AD, who attempted to make some sort of botanical sense out of these magical plants which have become the root of modern medicine.

The first British herbal, the Leech Book of Bald, was compiled by a friend of the famous King Alfred, who is said to have burnt a batch of cakes in 950. The best known herbal of all is probably that of Gerard who published his book in 1597 but was later accused of plagiarism - it is believed to have been compiled by somebody else. Culpeper, almost a century later, went one step further in herbalism and combined astrology with plants for the first time. In his day, all that apothecaries had to work with were plants, and many a homemaker was her own amateur herbalist making up simple cures for everyday ailments.

What has made herbs stand the test of time? It is surely their infinite variety, not just in their use in cookery, medicine, and beauty but also color, shape, and scent. To tend a herb garden today is to keep in touch with history, knowing that the plants we work with were used centuries ago and are rooted in legends and myths. So whether you are cooking with marjoram and mint, or picking bright marigolds for a table decoration, you know you are in touch with time.

*A herbal trio: marigold flowers partnered by mint and*

Mentha spicata · Calendula officinalis · Origanum majorana

Origanum majorana · Mentha spicata · Calendula officinalis

*Marjoram comes in several decorative guises.*

# INTRODUCING MARJORAM

MARJORAM IS one of the oldest herbs that is in general use today. A native plant of the Mediterranean region, the Greeks gave it its name *oros* and *ganos* which means "joy of the mountains." It was said to have been created by Aphrodite the goddess of love, whose touch gave marjoram its sweet spicy perfume. Not surprisingly, Greek couples often wore crowns of marjoram when they married, and wreaths of marjoram were laid on the dead to ensure they went to a happy life in the next world. Another myth claims that the King of Cyprus punished a servant for dropping a jar of perfume by turning him into a marjoram plant.

In ancient Egypt, marjoram was used as a disinfectant and to help preserve mummies in their tombs, but it was the Romans who spread it all over Europe.

Marjoram was described by Shakespeare as a "herb of grace." It was one of the many herbs used to protect people from the Plague. Sweet marjoram was used in Tudor times as an edging for knot gardens, its oil was also used to polish furniture and floors. Marjoram oil is much prized in some countries to rub on aching rheumaticky joints, to cure toothache, and soothe morning sickness. Aromatherapists use the essential oil for a relaxing massage.

There is not just one, but a whole family of marjorams, all with the same spicy, slightly sweet taste of varying intensity, according to which part of Europe, North Africa, or America they come from. It is the sun, or absence of it, that makes a great deal of difference to the pungency of marjoram's flavor.

There are many strange myths about marjoram. Gerard, the herbalist, said that an herb tea of marjoram would benefit those who "are given to overmuch sighing." Portuguese children believe to this day that if you sniff marjoram your nose will drop off. Tortoises are said to chew it to fortify themselves before a fight. Back in ancient times, Aristotle remarked that these curious creatures used it as an antidote to poisoning.

13

### COMMON OR WILD MARJORAM
### *Origanum vulgare*

This is a tough little plant which can be found growing wild on chalky downland. It is basically the same plant as the oregano of Italy and dittany of Greece, and it is used extensively in Mexico, too, where it is highly prized in cooking.

Marjoram can also be found in "crickle leaf," *Variegata* and the attractive golden *Aureum* forms.

### SWEET MARJORAM
### *Origanum marjorana*

A perennial plant with tiny white or blue flowers, which is grown as an annual in most parts of the country as it will not survive winter frosts. Its flavor is less bitter, more refined. Its small leaves have a distinctive, knotty growth and the plant has bright red stems.

ABOVE *The golden marjoram,*
*Origanum vulgare* "Aureum."

14

### POT MARJORAM
*Origanum onites*

This plant tends to spread quickly as it is more robust and bushier than sweet marjoram. It will usually survive the winter in cool climates. It has a slightly stronger flavor than sweet marjoram and produces white, pink, or mauve flowers in high summer.

This little herb can also be found in golden- and curly-leaved versions and is a very attractive prostrate ground-covering plant.

### DITTANY OF CRETE
*Origanum dictamnus*

This prostrate plant has leaves covered in whitish down and makes a good choice to grow in a confined space or on a rockery. It is not really suitable for cooking, but is taken as an herb tea in Crete, the Mediterranean island for which it is named.

ABOVE *Marjoram grows well in decorative pots.*

15

Origanum majorana · Mentha spicata · Calendula officinalis · Mentha spicata · Calendula officinalis · Origanum majorana · Mentha spicata · Calendula officinalis · Origanum majorana · Mentha spicata · Calendula officinalis · Origanum majorana

MARJORAM, MINT, AND MARIGOLD

# INTRODUCING MINT

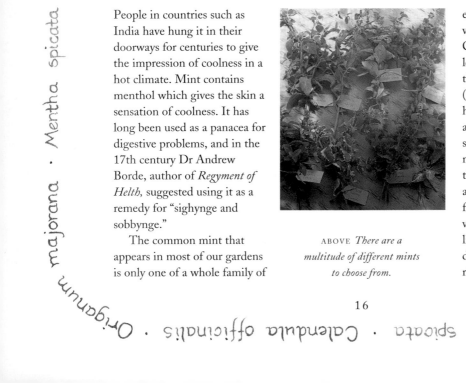

MINT HAS been held in high esteem throughout the centuries, being much prized in the Middle East and especially in North Africa, where it is used extensively for mint tea. The name comes from the beautiful nymph, Minta, who was pursued by Hades, the god of the underworld. His jealous wife, Persephone, cursed the maiden and turned her into a plant destined to live in the shade – a place that mint prefers to this day. For this reason it makes good ground cover in shady places.

People in countries such as India have hung it in their doorways for centuries to give the impression of coolness in a hot climate. Mint contains menthol which gives the skin a sensation of coolness. It has long been used as a panacea for digestive problems, and in the 17th century Dr Andrew Borde, author of *Regyment of Helth,* suggested using it as a remedy for "sighynge and sobbynge."

The common mint that appears in most of our gardens is only one of a whole family of

ABOVE *There are a multitude of different mints to choose from.*

eighteen or more different varieties ranging from Corsican mint, with tiny leaves and prostrate habit, to the so-called Irish mint (*Mentha raripila rubra*) which has dark red-tinged leaves and actually makes a red mint sauce. There is even a water mint (*Mentha aquatica*) which thrives in marshy conditions and has the same strong flavor as the others. The variegated versions of mint like *Mentha gentilis* are decorative plants in their own right in any flowerbed.

### SPEARMINT
*Mentha spicata*

This is the most popular variety for cooking. In England, it is made into a sauce and served with lamb. The oil is used to flavor chewing gum. There is also a curly version, *Crispata*.

### APPLE MINT
*Mentha rotundifolia*

This mint has furry, rounded leaves, and is often used in cooking. It has a slight but distinctive flavor of apple, hence its name. "Bowles Mint" (*M. rotundifolia* var. Bowles) has a particularly good flavor for mint sauce and is not as subject to the rust disease as other mints.

### PEPPERMINT
*Mentha piperita*

This mint is too pungent for mint sauce, but is often used in confectionery and in Crème de Menthe liqueur. It is also distilled to make peppermint oil.

### GINGER MINT
*Mentha gentilis*

This mint has attractive variegated leaves splashed with yellow.

### EAU-DE-COLOGNE MINT
*Mentha citrata* var eau de cologne

This mint has a fragrant, lemony taste and is used a great deal in potpourris and in versions of mint tea.

### PENNYROYAL
*Mentha pulegium*

Has a strong flavor, which is unsuitable for cooking, but it is used in medicine. It is an abortifacient and should be taken with great care. Grow pennyroyal for decoration not for the table.

ABOVE *Look out for mint at farmers' markets.*

The true marigold has deep orange flowers.

# INTRODUCING MARIGOLD

MARIGOLD IS a flower of the sun. It came from India (where it is traditionally used to crown the statues of Hindu gods and to decorate their temples), and from Persia where it was first used in food. It reached this country via southern Europe, but takes happily to our climate. Its official name, calendula, comes from the Latin *calend*, meaning calender, because it was believed to flower on the first day of every month. Indeed, it flowers almost all year round in warm climates.

The "pot marigold" as the true marigold is sometimes called, is much appreciated as a herb as well as a flower. It has been used in household dyes, in butters, and to give a rich tone to casseroles and stews. But it has healing and antiseptic properties too. In the American Civil War wounds were treated with marigold leaves, and in the First World War, when medicines became in short supply, a paste of calendula was used on the wounds of soldiers. The sap of marigold is also said to soothe bee and wasp stings. The ancient Egyptians believed it would rejuvenate the skin, and it has been rediscovered today and used in many ranges of natural cosmetics.

Marigold has always been a flower of love and was used in magic spells to bewitch people.

Early herbals say that just looking at marigold will "drive evil humour out of the head." Gerard the herbalist noted that it was used in "Dutchland against Winter for broths and Physicall potions." Its bright petals are called "poor man's saffron" with good reason for they impart a yellow coloring to food when cooked.

If you are growing it for flavor be sure to get the true marigold – *Calendula*, rather than the African or French hybrids – *Tagetes*.

# PLANT CARE

*Clip pot – grown mints and marjorams frequently to keep them bushy.*

## MARJORAM
### *Origanum*

This herb grows to a height of up to 12 inches depending on the variety. It needs a sunny situation and a well-drained soil, preferring one that is alkaline (chalky.) It tends to become woody at the base with leggy shoots, so it should be trimmed back from time to time and some of the dead wood cut away. Divide up over-large clumps, since if it becomes tough and overgrown its flavor tends to deteriorate. Pull off some pieces of root in the fall, pot them, and bring them indoors to grow undercover and give you winter greenery.

## MINT
### *Mentha*

A perennial plant which grows up to 2 feet high from creeping roots which spread very rapidly and, if you are not careful, can soon take over a corner of the garden. Mint will grow almost anywhere in the garden and enjoys the shade. If you are short of space, it is best to plant it in a bottomless bucket sunk in the ground. Mint is best grown from pieces of root or cuttings, as it does not always come true to form if you start it from seed. Snip the plants frequently and pinch out the flowers to keep the plants bushy and encourage plenty of young growth which is what you need. Bring one or two roots indoors and grow the plant in pots to give you supplies of fresh mint in mid-winter.

*1. To keep mint from encroaching on the plants around it, take the bottom out of a tin or bucket, sink it in the ground, then plant the mint in the center.*

## MARIGOLD
### *Calendula officinalis*

Marigold is a hardy annual, grown each year from seed and reaching a height of up to 24 inches. It prefers the sun and will grow in almost any soil as long as it is not waterlogged. Sow marigold in the spring in a sunny place and thin the seedlings out to 10 inches apart. Or start it off in pots in the fall or sow it, one seed at a time, in divided seedtrays, transferring the seedlings to pots later on. Once fully established, marigold will go on to seed itself from year to year.

*1. To sow marigolds, put several seeds in a pot, and cover them with potting mixture. Keep the soil moist at all times.*

*2. When the seedlings are large enough to handle, transfer them carefully into individual pots.*

# HARVESTING

P ICK YOUR herbs early in the growing season to encourage them to produce vigorous new growth. The leaves of mint and marjoram should be taken before the plant starts to flower otherwise the flavor will be less strong. Choose only the best parts of the plant and gather them on a dry day, after the morning dew has dried.

### HARVESTING MARJORAM

When harvesting marjoram, do not cut into the woody growth for material to use or dry, only do so if you are pruning it back. Cut back marjoram well before the first frosts appear, or the plant may be weakened by the weather. If you treat marjoram carefully, you should be able to pick some shoots through the winter.

### HARVESTING MINT

You should be able to harvest your mint at least three times during the growing season. The first crop will be the best. Cut mint well back at the end of the summer and don't leave the dying stems on the plants. Nip off flowering shoots as they appear, as they rob the plant of its essential oils.

### HARVESTING MARIGOLDS

Pick the flowers of marigold just as they fully open. Leave the blooms for about half an hour before taking the petals off, then they will come away from the center more easily. If you are picking whole marigold flowers for drying, cut off the stem as well, don't leave a stump. If you are collecting marigold seed, make sure that it is brown and fully ripe before you raid the plants. Removing the seed heads will encourage more blooms.

22

*Marigold petals make a vivid display.*

MARJORAM, MINT, AND MARIGOLD

*Mint and marjoram hanging up to dry.*

24

MARJORAM, MINT, AND MARIGOLD

# DRYING YOUR HERBS

W HEN DRYING herbs make sure that this is done as quickly as possible. Choose somewhere that has a good flow of air to get rid of moisture as speedily as you can. Once dry, the herbs should be stored immediately in a dark place. Avoid any contact with moisture as the herbs will re-absorb it and become musty.

Hang marigold flowers up by their stems to dry, suspending them from a rack or fine chicken wire so that they do not touch each other.

Spread marigold petals on paper in a warm, dark place, spacing them out. As soon as they are crisp and dry, put them in opaque jars or airtight containers. If they are in clear jars they should be stored away from the light or they will lose their color.

Keep harvested marigold seed in paper bags or envelopes ready for re-sowing.

*1. Put a layer of silica gel crystals in a covered container, place the marigolds carefully on top, then cover completely with more crystals. Add the lid and leave for 4–5 days to dry.*

Mint can be dried in bunches, hung in a warm dark place. Do not leave it too long – the moment that the leaves turn crisp, crumble them onto a sheet of paper, then store them in jars or airtight containers. The leaves can also be frozen very successfully in plastic sandwich bags. Or you can mince them, ready for cooking and drinks, and freeze in sections in an icetray. Decant the cubes when they are fully frozen and store them in a bag in the freezer.

Marjoram can be dried in bunches but is best done sprig by sprig, laid out on paper on a wire rack. If you dry them in bunches, once the leaves are crisp, plunge the bunch into a paper bag and strip off the leaves.

Marjoram can also be frozen, but releases its flavor best by being preserved in oil or vinegar.

# A HERBAL ROCK GARDEN

A HERB ROCKERY makes a marvellous way to show off smaller, shrubbier plants, such as marjoram. So if you already have a rock garden, consider converting it to aromatics. You'll find that the prostrate varieties work well.

A garden like this is ideal for Mediterranean plants like thyme, marjoram, and sage, which will knit together to make a carpet of color. The rocks will shelter shade-loving plants and also help to keep the roots of stronger growers like mint under control. Choose prostrate versions of plants as much as possible – dittany of Crete (*Origanum dictamnus*) looks particularly good in a rockery setting and so does golden marjoram. And tiny creeping mints, like pennyroyal and Corsican mint, will give a contrasting dark green color.

*1.* *Start by making a mound of soil. Dig in plenty of good compost or add fertilizer. Make the mound rounded rather than sharp. If you are short of stones, try making a rockery in a corner which can be very effective. Push your rocks well in place in the soil.*

*2.* *Using a trowel, put your plants in place then scatter gravel evenly over the surface.*

### A MINI-LAWN

*Make a miniature lawn on the top of a rocky outcrop, using Corsican mint. Given the minimum of soil it will form an attractive tiny green carpet.*

# A KITCHEN PLANTER

ROW HERBS in the kitchen too. Provided you have a sunny window they are certain to thrive. Bring pieces of plant in at the end of the summer and they will go on growing for you through the winter. Marigolds will continue to flower, basil will thrive, and you'll have supplies of fresh marjoram and mint to cut at Christmas time.

One of the most attractive types of container for herbs is a classic soup tureen or punch bowl. You can then take the tureen to the table when serving a salad and encourage guests to snip off the herb of their choice. Marjoram, especially the curly-leaved and golden kinds, and mint, grow well in tureens. Add chives, parsley, thyme, and basil. The plants can be dug up from the garden, used for a while, and then returned to their former site while you bring in a fresh supply.

*1. Choose appropriate containers for the purpose. Look out at yard sales for large old pieces of tableware – they make ideal herb planters.*

*2. Remember that you don't have to choose something with drainage holes. Use the container as a cache-pot instead: keep the herbs in their pots and stand them inside it, then scatter vermiculite or shredded bark over and in between them.*

*Marigold heads make an
ideal floating table*

## CUT HERBS FOR DECORATION

FLOWER ARRANGERS very often overlook herbs when they are searching for foliage. This is a pity, since they can add not only variety but perfume too, to a bouquet. With colors ranging from the near blue of rue to the vivid lime green of young tansy leaves and the gold of marjoram "Aureum" there is a whole host of shades to choose from. Look out for variegated varieties of mint and sage too, to complete the selection, edging the bouquet perhaps with the feathery fronds of dill or fennel. Freshly cut herbs, with all their variety of colors, make attractive kitchen posies to give to your hostess if you are invited for a meal. Wrap the stalks in a damp paper towel and cover with foil to keep them fresh. Try putting whole marigold flower heads in a bowl of water with floating candles. They make a marvellous centerpiece for a dinner table.

TIP
Try making a necklace of marigold flowers to go round the base of a candle, thread them on to cotton, or simply sit them in place.

## A HERB HANGING BASKET

PLANT UP this unusual hanging basket with several different kinds of marjoram and marigolds. You can suspend it on fine chains or, if you prefer, sit it on a worktop. Buy the largest-sized colander you can find. Paint it in the color of your choice – white looks good against green foliage, turquoise gives your container a Mediterranean look. Use an enamel paint if the colander is a metal one, or an acrylic paint if it is made from plastic.

*1. Line the colander with black plastic sheeting. Make one or two drainage holes in the bottom, using a large knitting needle or skewer. Fill the colander with compost, leaving a small dip in the middle.*

*2. Plant with several different varieties of marjoram. You can, if you like, poke one or two rooted cuttings through the holes in the sides to grow during the summer.*

# HERB SALADS

USE MARJORAM, mint, and marigold for tasty salads,
homing in on Mediterranean leaves like radicchio and
the peppery rocket. Chop the marjoram and mint,
and scatter marigold petals on top for extra color.

*Origanum majorana · Mentha spicata · Calendula officinalis · Mentha spicata · Calendula officinalis · Origanum majorana · Calendula officinalis · Mentha spicata · Origanum majorana · Calendula officinalis · Mentha spicata · Origanum*

MARJORAM, MINT, AND MARIGOLD

# MINT AND CUCUMBER SALAD

MINT AND CUCUMBER make a perfect partnership. Try this cooling side salad or appetizer, substituting yogurt for the vinaigrette if you wish.

### INGREDIENTS

**Serves 4**

*1 cucumber*

*⅔ cup vinaigrette*

*2 tbs chopped mint*

❖ Peel the cucumber and slice it very thinly. Sprinkle the slices with salt, and put in a colander set over a plate.

❖ Put a weight on top and leave the cucumber to drain for 30 minutes.

❖ Transfer to a serving dish and pour on the vinaigrette, then top with the chopped mint.

❖ Leave to marinate for a further 30 minutes before serving.

TIP
If your cucumber slices look limp, put them in iced water for a while to revive them.

# TOMATO AND MARJORAM SALAD

YOU CAN substitute the more pungent oregano for marjoram in this salad. If you use the herb in dried form, halve the quantity.

### INGREDIENTS

**Serves 4**

*1 clove garlic*

*⅔ cup vinaigrette*

*4 large tomatoes*

*3tbs finely grated Parmesan cheese*

*1 tbs chopped marjoram*

❖ Make several slits in the garlic clove and put it in the vinaigrette.

❖ Leave for at least 1 hour, and preferably overnight.

❖ Slice the tomatoes and put them in a shallow dish. Season well with salt and pepper and sprinkle with the Parmesan.

❖ Remove the garlic clove from the vinaigrette and pour the dressing over the tomatoes.

❖ Top with the chopped marjoram and serve with warm, crusty bread.

MARJORAM, MINT, AND MARIGOLD

# MIXED HERB BREAD

THE FASHION for unusual and interesting breads has revived the ancient idea of adding herbs to the dough. Use one herb only or make a mix. Add marigold petals too, if you like, to give added flavor and a golden coloring.

INGREDIENTS

**Makes 1 x 1¹/₂ pound loaf**

2 cups all-purpose flour

2 cups wholewheat flour

2 tsp salt

1 tsp dried marjoram

1 tsp dried mint

1 tsp butter or margarine

2 tsp chopped marjoram

2 tsp chopped mint

2 tsp sugar

1¹/₄ cups warm water

2 tsp active dry yeast

❖ In a large, warmed bowl, mix the flours together with the salt and the dried herbs. Rub in the fat, then stir in the chopped fresh herbs.

❖ Dissolve the sugar in about half the warm water, and sprinkle the yeast on top. Leave for about ten minutes, until frothy.

❖ Make a hollow in the center of the flour and pour in the yeast mixture. Gradually mix with the flour, adding the remaining warm water. Finish mixing by hand until you have a soft dough.

❖ Knead the dough thoroughly on a floured board. Mold into 2 rounds, braids, or coils, and place on a baking tray. Cover with oiled plastic wrap or wax paper and leave in a warm place for about 1 hour to double in size.

❖ Bake on the middle shelf of a preheated oven at 450 degrees for 30–40 minutes or until the bread sounds hollow when tapped.

# MARIGOLD BREAD ROLLS

**B**READ ROLLS are quick and easy to make, and freeze well for future use. Get some out of the freezer overnight and they will thaw out nicely to serve for breakfast. The marigold petals in this recipe give the dough an attractive color.

### INGREDIENTS

**Makes 12**

*1 tsp sugar*
*½ cup tepid milk*
*1½ tsp active dry yeast*
*2 cups all-purpose flour*
*1 tsp salt*
*4 tbs butter or margarine*
*1 tbs tightly packed marigold petals*
*2 eggs, beaten*
*marigold petals, to decorate*

❖ Dissolve the sugar in the milk, sprinkle the yeast over it, and leave to froth.
❖ Mix the flour with the salt, rub in the fat, then mix in the marigold petals.
❖ Add the milk and half the beaten eggs. Mix until it forms a smooth dough, adding a little more milk if necessary.
❖ Place on a floured board, cover with oiled plastic wrap or wax paper, and leave in a warm place for about 1 hour until doubled in size.

❖ Knead the dough lightly, then cut it into 12 pieces. Shape each piece into a roll and put in rows on a greased baking sheet. Return to a warm place and allow the rolls to rise again for 20 minutes.
❖ Brush the rolls with the beaten egg, and sprinkle marigold petals on top. Bake in a preheated oven at 425 degrees for about 15 minutes. The rolls should sound hollow when tapped.

# BARBECUES

**B**ARBECUES CAN become gourmet feasts if you use herbs to flavor the food. Lay sprigs of marjoram in and among charbroiled vegetables, especially peppers and eggplant. Press mint into fish as you broil it, and wind marjoram around lamb kebobs to give a hint of flavor. Use herbs on barbecued burgers too, to give them an outdoor taste.

# MINTED BARBECUE BURGERS

**M**AKE YOUR own barbecue burgers. They cook more quickly than chunks of meat and give you endless scope for ingenuity. The mint used here could be replaced by marjoram for a different flavor. Or you could substitute cooked puréed pulses and finely chopped vegetables for the meat.

INGREDIENTS

**Makes 8**

*2 cups ground beef*

*2 tbs minced mint*

*pinch of ground nutmeg*

*1 slice white bread*

*1 beaten egg*

*4 tbs butter*

*6 mint sprigs, to garnish*

❖ In a mixing bowl, combine the beef, mint, and nutmeg. Season well.

❖ Moisten the bread in a little milk or water, then add to the beef mixture with the egg, stirring well.

❖ Shape the mix into burgers ¾ inch thick.

❖ Brown the burgers quickly on both sides on the barbecue. Shift away from intense heat and continue cooking for up to 5 minutes or until thoroughly cooked through.

❖ Serve very hot, topped with the butter and a garnish of fresh mint sprigs.

TIP

Use a bunch of mint to baste barbecue food with oil. The leaves will add a hint of flavor to the meat.

MARJORAM, MINT, AND MARIGOLD

# RICH BEEF CASEROLE WITH MARIGOLD

COPY THE medieval housewife and put some marigold petals in your casseroles. They will help to give a rich brown color and add a delicate yet distinctive flavor.

### INGREDIENTS
**Serves 4**
*1½ pounds chuck steak*
*1 large onion*
*2 green peppers*
*2 tbs oil*
*⅔ cup red wine*
*2 tbs tomato paste*
*2 tbs freshly picked marigold petals*

❖ Cut the meat into small cubes. Peel and slice the onion, seed and slice the peppers. Heat the oil in a skillet and sauté the onion until golden brown. Remove with a slotted spoon and place in a casserole. Fry the peppers until they have wilted, then add them to the onion. Brown the meat on all sides. Pour on the wine, stir in the tomato paste, and bring to the boil. Add to the casserole, add the marigold petals, and stir well.
❖ Cover and cook in a preheated oven at 325 degrees for about 2½ hours.

# PORK PROVENÇAL WITH MARJORAM

THE COMBINATION of slivers of orange peel and the marjoram gives this slow-cooked dish a delicious flavor.

### INGREDIENTS
*2 onions*
*1 green pepper*
*1 red pepper*
*1 cup mushrooms*
*2 tbs all-purpose flour*
*1½ pounds sliced pork fillet*
*4 tbs olive oil*
*1½ cups canned tomatoes*
*2 strips orange peel*
*1 tbs minced marjoram*

❖ Peel and slice the onions, seed and slice the peppers, and slice the mushrooms. Season the flour with salt and pepper, and coat the slices of pork in it. Fry the onions in the oil, then add the pork and fry until browned. Remove with a slotted spoon and put into a casserole. Fry the peppers and mushrooms until tender, then add the tomatoes. Transfer to the casserole, add the orange peel, and marjoram.
❖ Cover and cook in a preheated oven at 350 degrees for 1½ hours.

# HERB CHEESES

Liven up ordinary cream cheeses by adding handfuls of herbs. Not only do they taste good but look very decorative too. Try soft goat's cheese for extra flavor. If you are using a curd cheese, mix it to a smooth paste in a food processor first.

## ROLLED HERB CHEESE

### INGREDIENTS

**Makes 1 cup**
*1 cup pot or cream cheese*
*handful of chopped mint, marjoram, or other herbs*
*long stems of chives (optional)*

❖ Beat the cheese well. Using your hands, shape it into small flattened rounds.
❖ Put mounds of the chopped herb on a board and roll the cheeses thoroughly in it until they are completely covered. Tie them up into little parcels, using the chives.
❖ Keep the cheeses in a cool place for at least 24 hours before serving, to allow the flavor to permeate.

## TWO-TONE MARIGOLD CHEESE

### INGREDIENTS

**Makes 1 cup**
*4 ounces Colby or Jack cheese*
*1/3 cup pot or cream cheese*
*3 tbs marigold petals*
*marigold petals or flowers, to garnish*

❖ Grate the Colby or Jack cheese coarsely, then mix together with the soft cheese and the marigold petals.
❖ Chill the mixture in a refrigerator.
❖ Shape into small flattened rounds, and roll in more marigold petals. Or make into larger rounds and top each with a marigold flower.

### TIP

If you are making a herb cheese, allow the basic ingredient – Cheddar, Cheshire or soft cheese – to reach room temperature before you work with it. If it is particularly cold you could put it in the microwave on defrost for a second or two.

MARJORAM, MINT, AND MARIGOLD

MARJORAM, MINT, AND MARIGOLD

# GOLDEN MARIGOLD CAKE

SE MARIGOLD petals to give a golden color and subtle taste to cakes and cookies. You can, if you prefer, use dried marigold petals that have been crushed to a powder.

INGREDIENTS

**Makes 1 x 6-inch cake**

*2 cups self-rising flour*
*pinch of salt*
*1/2 cup butter or margarine*
*1/2 cup superfine sugar*
*1 beaten egg*
*juice of 1 small lemon*
*6 tbs milk*
*2 tbs freshly picked*
*marigold petals*
*marigold petals, to decorate*

❖ Sift the flour and salt into a mixing bowl, and rub in the fat until the mixture looks like fine breadcrumbs. Stir in the sugar. Make a well in the center, and pour in the egg and the lemon juice. Gradually work in the dry ingredients, adding the milk a little at a time, until you have a mix of dropping consistency.

❖ Fold in the marigold petals and turn the mixture into a 6-inch cake pan. Bake in a preheated oven at 350 degrees for about 1¼ hours or until golden and firm to the touch. Turn out and cool on a wire rack, then serve decorated with marigold petals.

# MARIGOLD HEARTH CAKES

INGREDIENTS

**Makes about 12**

*1/2 cup butter*
*2 cups self-rising flour*
*1/3 cup brown sugar*
*1 beaten egg*
*1tbs chopped marigold petals*

❖ Rub the butter into the flour, and mix in the sugar. Stir in the beaten egg, then fold in the marigold petals.

❖ Roll out the dough and cut it into thin rounds.

❖ Cook on a griddle or in a heavy skillet over a low heat for 2–3 minutes until the cakes have risen and turned golden.

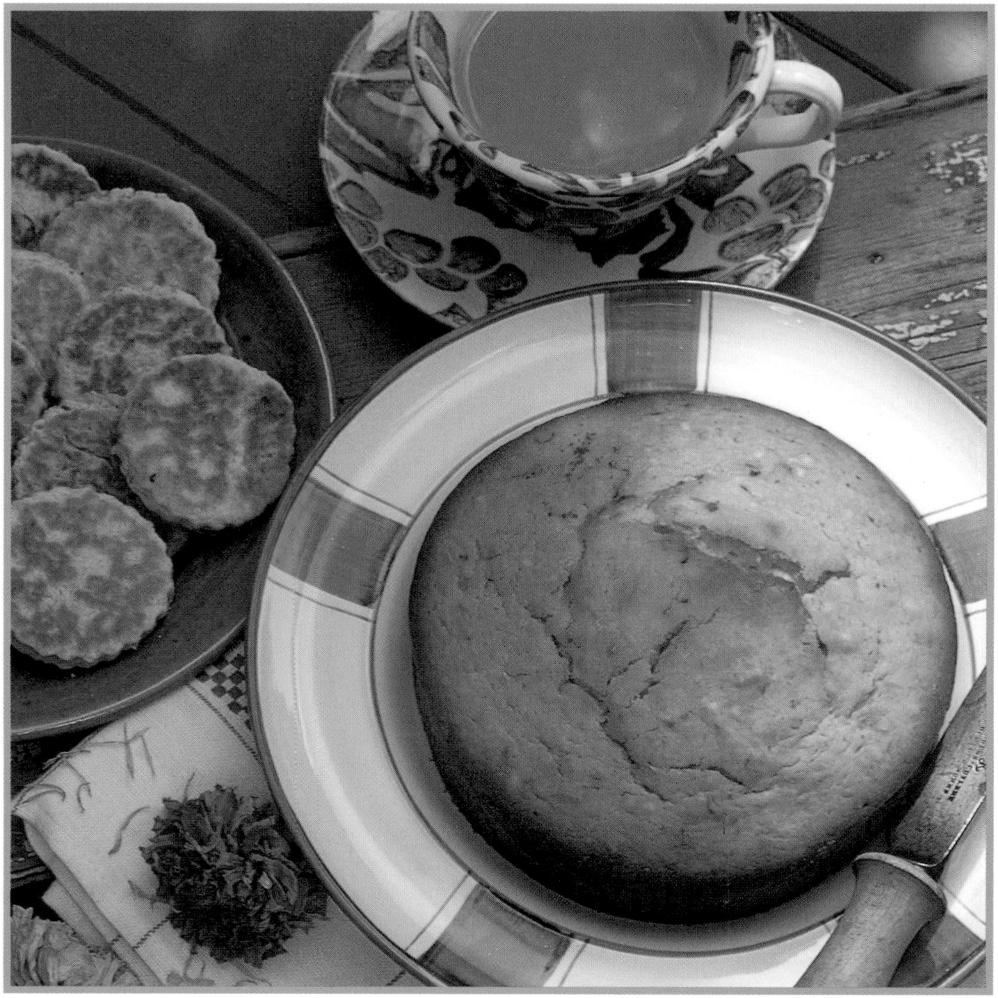

# MINT
# CANDIES

 LD-FASHIONED peppermint patties are easy to make if you have a candy thermometer.

INGREDIENTS

**Makes 1 pound**

*⅔ cup water*

*2 cups granulated sugar*

*pinch of cream of tartar*

*1 tbs butter*

*4 drops oil of peppermint*

❖ Put the water in a pan, add the sugar, and let it dissolve slowly over a low heat. Bring the mixture to the boil, add a good pinch of cream of tartar, and boil to 240 degrees. Allow to cool a little, then stir in the butter.

❖ Sprinkle a little water into a large earthenware bowl, pour the sugar syrup on to it, and leave to cool for 15 minutes. When a skin starts to form round the edge, sprinkle the oil of peppermint over the mixture. Using a metal spoon "stir" the mixture in a figure-of-eight, pushing the outside towards the center.

❖ As the mixture becomes grainy and opaque, turn it out onto a sheet of nonstick baking paper. Knead it, then roll out to a ½-inch thickness. Cut into shapes with small cookie or candy cutters.

# CHOCOLATE
# MINT LEAVES

OME-MADE candies have a charm all of their own and are surprisingly easy to make, even if you have never tried them before. Chocolate-covered mint leaves make marvellous confectionery to serve with coffee after a meal in place of storebought mints. Keep them fresh in the refrigerator.

INGREDIENTS

*1 egg white*

*superfine sugar*

*handful of young peppermint leaves*

*8 squares (8 ounces) dark Baker's chocolate*

❖ Whisk the egg white until it is opaque. Make sure the leaves are completely dry, then, using an artist's brush, paint each leaf with egg white, holding it by the stalk. Dip into superfine sugar, then lay the coated mint leaves to dry on nonstick baking paper on a wire rack.

❖ When the leaves have dried completely, melt the chocolate in a double boiler. Take each leaf by the stalk, dip into the melted chocolate, and put to dry on a fresh sheet of nonstick baking paper.

TIP

If you want to make plain chocolate leaves, simply lay the untreated mint leaves on a plate, paint them with melted chocolate on one side only, then strip the leaf off when they are dry. The impression of the leaf will remain.

MARJORAM, MINT, AND MARIGOLD

## MINT LIQUEUR

S ERVE THIS unusual liqueur well chilled in small glasses as an after-dinner drink, or try it as an apéritif with tasty morsels of smoked fish. Toss it back, Russian style, in one shot.

INGREDIENTS

**Makes 1 quart**

*1 cup tightly packed peppermint leaves*

*1 quart vodka*

*100 g (4 oz) sugar*

❖ Put the mint in a wide-necked jar, and cover with the vodka.

❖ Put on the lid, shake well, then leave to steep for 2 weeks.

❖ Add the sugar and steep for 2 more weeks, shaking the jar from time to time to dissolve the sugar.

❖ Strain the liqueur into a fresh bottle, add a sprig of mint for decoration.

❖ Leave for a further 2 weeks before drinking.

## MINT JULEP

INGREDIENTS

**Makes 3¼ cups**

*⅔ cup water*

*4 tbs chopped mint*

*2 tbs sugar*

*juice of 1 lemon*

*2 cups sparkling mineral water*

*½ cup bourbon*

❖ Boil the water and pour it over the mint. Add the sugar and stir until dissolved. Add the lemon juice, then leave the mixture to cool.

❖ Strain into a jug, stir in the mineral water and the whisky. Pour on to ice cubes in tall glasses, add a sprig of mint and serve.

# MINT TEA

TIP

The best mint
to use is Moroccan
mint (*Mentha
viridis.*) Failing that,
use peppermint.
Sometimes in winter
the Moroccans add
sweet marjoram
to the mint.

INGREDIENTS

**Makes 3 ³/₄ cups**
*1¹/₂ tbs green tea (available from
specialist tea suppliers)
handful of whole mint leaves
³/₄ cup lump sugar*

❖ Rinse out a teapot with boiling water. Put in
the tea and cover with the mint. Add the sugar
and fill the teapot with boiling water.
❖ Leave to draw for 5 minutes, taking care that the
mint does not rise above the surface of the water.
❖ Pour out into small glasses.
❖ In Morocco they make two pots of tea at a
time and pour the liquid from both pots at the
same time into the glasses.

MARJORAM, MINT, AND MARIGOLD

# MINT AND MARROW CHUTNEY

**T**HIS TRADITIONAL chutney can be made substituting zucchini for squash if they are easier to obtain.

INGREDIENTS

**Makes 4 pounds**

*3 pounds winter squash*

*1 cup shallots*

*1/2 pound apples*

*12 peppercorns*

*3/4 in piece ginger root*

*1 cup yellow raisins*

*1 packed cup brown sugar*

*3 3/4 cups malt vinegar*

*handful of mint*

❖ Peel and seed the squash, and cut into small pieces. Place in a bowl, sprinkle with salt, cover, and leave overnight. Peel and slice the shallots. Peel, core, and slice the apples. Rinse the squash, drain well, then place in a pan with the shallots and apples. Tie the peppercorns and the ginger in cheesecloth and add to the pan together with the sultanas, sugar, and vinegar. Chop the mint and add to the pan.

❖ Bring to the boil, reduce the heat, then simmer until the consistency is thick and there is no excess liquid. Put into warmed sterilized pots and seal.

# RAITA

**T**HIS COOLING fresh relish made from mint, cucumber, and yogurt can be stored in the refrigerator for a few days. Serve with curries.

INGREDIENTS

**Serves 6**

*2 tbs mint*

*6-inch piece of cucumber*

*2 1/2 cups thick-set yogurt*

*1/2 tsp cumin seeds*

*1/4 tsp cayenne or chili powder*

❖ Finely chop the mint. Peel and coarsely grate the cucumber.

❖ Whisk the yogurt in a bowl until creamy, add all the other ingredients and mix again. Season with plenty of salt and some black pepper.

❖ Cover and leave in the refrigerator for at least a day before eating to allow the flavors to permeate the yogurt.

TIP

Mint adds a delicious flavor to preserves of all kinds – try adding mint leaves to apple jelly for instance.

# PAINTED HERB POTS

MARIGOLDS make stunning decorative motifs with their bright and colorful blooms. With a little practice, you can paint the flowers freehand to decorate terracotta plant pots, or embellish an old enamel breadbox or a set of storage canisters for the kitchen. When painting in such a free way, spontaneity is more important than precision, so try painting some flowers first on waste paper until you get the hang of it and build up your confidence.

MATERIALS

*piece of natural sponge
acrylic paints in bright
blue and an assortment of
yellow, orange, red, and
brown shades
flat brush*

**TIP**
Don't restrict your artistry to flowers – suns, moons, and rainbows are equally attractive. Collect inspiring images from magazines and books.

*1. Using an old plate or a piece of waste paper as a palette, squeeze out some blue paint, and add a little water to it. Dab the sponge into the paint and lightly press the sponge all over the pot to leave a mottled pattern. Leave to dry completely.*

*2. Squeeze blobs of yellow, orange, and red paint closely together on your palette. Mix them together slightly with the brush, so that the mixture is streaky and the overall color is a deep orange. Paint naive flower shapes on to the pot, with strips of streaky color radiating out from the center.*

*Leave to dry. Repeat the process again, painting a smaller flower in lighter tones within those already worked. Leave to dry.*

*3. To make the flower centers, dab the middles of the flowers a few times with the brush loaded with a deeper color. Leave to dry.*

MARJORAM, MINT, AND MARIGOLD

## TWO POTPOURRIS

P ERFUME YOUR house with potpourris. They're easy to make, so dry as many herbs as you can and have them to hand for making potpourris. Vary the ingredients to your own taste and what you have available, but always include the orris root as it "fixes" the scent and makes your potpourri last longer.

50

*Origanum majorana · Mentha spicata · Calendula officinalis · Mentha spicata · Calendula officinalis · Origanum majorana · Origanum majorana · Mentha spicata · Calendula officinalis*

MARJORAM, MINT, AND MARIGOLD

# MARJORAM, MARIGOLD, AND MINT

ARJORAM, marigold, and mint make a harmonious trio on which to base a potpourri. The spices – cloves and nutmeg – give it an exotic fragrance, while the orris root, which is derived from the white iris, preserves the perfume.

### INGREDIENTS

2½ cups mixed dried marjoram leaves and marigold petals
2½ cups mixed dried lemon balm and mint
¼ cup dried lavender
2 tbs dried rosemary
2 tbs dried orris root
½ cinnamon stick
1 strip dried lemon peel
½ tsp whole cloves
½ tsp grated nutmeg
3 drops rose geranium oil
2 drops lemon oil
1 drop peppermint oil
dried marigold flowers and mint leaves, to decorate

❖ Mix all the dry ingredients, then add the oils and stir.
❖ Decorate with whole dried marigold flowers and mint leaves.

# GOLDEN MARIGOLD MIX

THIS IS particularly colorful. Set it out in open bowls around the room, or stow away in fabric sachets.

### INGREDIENTS

2½ cups dried yellow and orange flowers
1¼ cups dried marigold petals
2 tbs mixed dried marjoram and thyme
2 tbs senna pods
2 tbs dried orris root
2 tsp ground cinnamon
2 broken cinnamon sticks
4 tbs chopped dried lemon and orange peel
4 drops marigold oil
2 drops orange oil
1 drop lemon oil
dried marigold flowers
2 dried orange slices
2 dried lemon slices

❖ Mix all the ingredients except the citrus slices, reserving some of the dried yellow and orange flowers to top the mix.
❖ Sprinkle with the oils, mix again, then top with yellow and orange flowers, whole dried marigold flowers, and the dried orange and lemon slices.

# CREAMS AND FRESHENERS

M arigold's healing properties come to the fore in cosmetic creams. You will find its Latin name, *calendula* mentioned in many old herbal recipes. Even if you don't want to make your own cosmetics, it is worth while stirring a strong infusion of fresh marigold petals into a storebought moisturizer to give it some of marigold's special qualities.

Origanum majorana · Mentha spicata · Calendula officinalis · Mentha spicata · Calendula officinalis · Origanum majorana ·

MARJORAM, MINT, AND MARIGOLD

# CALENDULA CREAM

THIS RICH cream is particularly soothing for the skin, particularly after sunburn. Use it last thing at night too, for a smooth, supple skin. The borax helps improve its keeping qualities. If you leave it out of the recipe, keep the cream in the refrigerator.

### INGREDIENTS

*1 tbs beeswax*
*1 tbs cocoa butter*
*1 tbs lanolin*
*1½ tbs marigold oil (see below right)*
*1 tsp glycerine*
*2 tbs strong infusion of marigold petals (see below)*
*¼ tsp borax*
*6 drops oil of petitgrain (optional)*

❖ Infuse a handful of marigold petals in half a cup of boiling water.
❖ Melt the beeswax, cocoa butter, and lanolin together in a double boiler or in the microwave on a low setting.
❖ Warm the marigold oil with the glycerine, then stir into the beeswax mix.
❖ Keeping the mixture warm, beat in the marigold infusion and the borax, then add the oil of petitgrain and beat again.
❖ Put into small sterilized jars.

# MINT FOOT FRESHENER

TRY THIS old recipe for tired feet. The natural oil in the mint has a cooling effect.

### INGREDIENTS

*large bunch of mint*
*10 cups boiling water*

❖ Immerse the mint in a saucepan of the boiling water. Allow to bubble for a minute or two, cover and leave to cool, then strain.
❖ Plunge your feet into this freshener while it is still tepid. Or keep the mix in a large pitcher in the fridge, and use it to sponge aching feet.

## MARIGOLD OR MARJORAM OIL

*You will need 1¼ cups marigold petals or marjoram leaves to 1¼ cups sunflower oil. Chop the petals or leaves finely, put into a wide-necked jar and cover with the oil which has been warmed slightly in a saucepan or in the microwave. Shake the bottle well and stand somewhere warm, such as a sunny windowsill. Leave for at least 2 weeks, then strain the oil into a fresh bottle.*

MARJORAM, MINT, AND MARIGOLD

# CONDITIONERS AND RINSES

 OME-MADE herbal conditioners and rinses are quick to make and much cheaper to produce than anything you could find in the stores. Try them – you will be impressed by the results.

## A MARIGOLD HAIR RINSE

 N INFUSION of marigold petals brightens blonde hair, giving it golden tones.

### INGREDIENTS

*handful of marigold petals*
*1¼ cups of water*
*2 tsp malt or cider vinegar*

❖ Boil the water, pour it over a bunch of petals then cool, drain, stir in the vinegar (which helps its keeping qualities) and bottle to have by you next time you wash your hair.

### TIP
If you are sitting out in the sun, give yourself an instant hair treatment by massaging herbal oil conditioner into your hair then covering it with a towel.

## HERBAL OIL HAIR CONDITIONER

EE HOW lustrous your hair looks after using this pre-shampoo conditioning treatment. The oil can be made up in large quantities and stored in a refrigerator, but shake it well before you use it.

### INGREDIENTS

*1 tbs marjoram oil (page 53)*
*1 tbs lemon juice*
*1 egg yolk*

❖ Mix the egg yolk with the lemon juice, beat in the marjoram oil then warm gently (in the microwave if you have one) before use.
❖ Massage the oil into your hair, cover with a plastic bathcap or plastic bag, then wrap your head in hot towels.
❖ Leave for at least 15 minutes, then shampoo thoroughly.

MARJORAM, MINT, AND MARIGOLD

# MINT WASH BALLS

IT'S SIMPLE to turn an ordinary cake of soap into a herbal one, provided you buy unscented soap for the purpose. This soap is adapted from a 16th century recipe.

INGREDIENTS

*1 tbs mint leaves*

*⅔ cup water*

*2 drops peppermint oil*

*5-ounce bar unscented soap*

❖ Chop the mint very finely. Bring the water to the boil, add the peppermint oil, then grate in the soap, reheating if necessary in a microwave or double boiler, until it has dissolved.

❖ Leave to cool for 15 minutes, then knead to a smooth paste.

❖ Turn out on to a board, sprinkle with chopped mint, knead and add more mint until it is all used up.

❖ Shape into small balls, wrap in plastic wrap and leave to dry for 3 days.

❖ Then re-wrap and leave for 1 month for the scent to permeate the soap before using.

TIP

Hand-made wash balls make an attractive present – wrap them in crumpled colored tissue paper. Mold them on to the end of a ribbon or cotton rope and they can be used in the shower too.

# MARIGOLD SOAP

THE HEALING qualities of marigold come into their own with this old-fashioned soap made with glycerine and honey. Make some and find out for yourself how gentle it is to the skin. It makes a good choice for a Christmas present, too.

INGREDIENTS

*2 tsp glycerine*

*handful of marigold leaves*

*5-ounce bar unscented saop*

*2 tsp clear honey*

*1. Warm the glycerine and steep the petals in it. Leave it to infuse for at least 1 hour. Grate the soap into a microwave-proof bowl and melt in the microwave on a low setting. Otherwise use a double boiler.*

*2. Beat in the glycerine/petal infusion and the honey. Pour into molds greased with a little oil.*

MARJORAM, MINT, AND MARIGOLD

MARJORAM, MINT, AND MARIGOLD

# KITCHEN SACHETS

MAKE THE MOST of marjoram's insect-repellent properties by growing plenty to make into kitchen sachets or herb bags for the wardrobe and linen closet. A few dried marigold petals add color and fragrance. In the Middle Ages, it was said that a bag containing a wolf's tooth and marigold petals wrapped in bay leaves, kept under the pillow at night, would enable you to see what burglars were up to in the dark.

MATERIALS

*rectangles of coarse linen or burlap 8 × 6 inches*
*handful of dried marjoram*
*small marigolds*

◈ Make up small bags with the linen or burlap, gluing the side and bottom.
◈ Fill with dried herbs and glue the top.
◈ Braid strands of linen or burlap to make loops for handles and stitch in place.
◈ Add a decorative bow.

TIP
If you use a really open-weave fabric like cheesecloth, you can add fresh marigolds to your herb-filled sachets and let them dry inside. Otherwise dry your marigolds in the usual way and crumble the petals.

MARJORAM, MINT, AND MARIGOLD

# INDEX

**A**
apple mint 17

**B**
barbecues 34
beef casserole 37
bread 32, 33
burgers 34

**C**
cakes 40
calendula 19, 52–3
candies 42
casseroles 37
cheeses 38
chocolate leaves 42
chutney 47
conditioners 54
Corsican mint 16, 26
creams 52–3

**D**
dittany of Crete 15, 26
drinks 44–5
drying herbs 25

**E**
eau-de-cologne mint 17

**F**
flower arrangements 29
foot freshener 53

**G**
ginger mint 17
golden marigold cake 40

**H**
hair care 54
hanging baskets 29
harvesting 22

**I**
Irish mint 16

**J**
julep 44

**K**
kitchen planter 27
kitchen sachets 58–9

**L**
lawns 26
liqueurs 44

**M**
marigold 19
    beef casserole 37
    bread 32, 33
    cakes 40
    cheese 38
    creams 52–3
    drying 25

    hair rinse 54
    hanging baskets 29
    harvesting 22
    kitchen planter 27
    kitchen sachets 58–9
    oil 53
    painted pots 48
    plant care 21
    potpourri 51

salads 30
soap 56
marjoram 13–15
    barbecues 34
    bread 32
    cheese 38
    conditioner 54
    drying 25
    hanging baskets 29
    harvesting 22
    kitchen planter 27
    kitchen sachets 58–9
    oil 53, 54
    plant care 20
    pork provençal 37
    potpourri 51
    salads 30–1
mini-lawns 26
mint 16–17
    barbecues 34
    bread 32
    candies 42
    cheese 38
    chocolate leaves 42
    drying 25
    foot freshener 53
    harvesting 22
    julep 44
    kitchen planter 27
    liqueur 44
    marrow chutney 47
    plant care 21
    potpourri 51
    raita 47
    salads 30–1
    tea 45
    wash balls 56

**O**
oils 53, 54

**P**
painted herb pots 48
pennyroyal 17, 26
peppermint 17
peppermint creams 42
plant care 20–1
pork provençal 37
pot marigold 19
pot marjoram 15
potpourris 50–1

**R**
raita 47
rinses 54
rock gardens 26

**S**
salads 30–1
soap 56
spearmint 17
sweet marjoram 14

**T**
tea 45
tomato and marjoram salad 31

**W**
wash balls 56
water mint 16
wild marjoram 14

Origanum majorana · Mentha spicata · Calendula officinalis

MARJORAM, MINT, AND MARIGOLD

# ACKNOWLEDGMENTS

The publishers would like to thank
the following companies for their help:

BASKETS AND GLASSWARE
*Global Village,*
*Sparrow Works, Bower Hinton, Martock, Somerset.*
*Telephone: (01935) 823390*

DRIED HERBS AND FLOWERS
*The Hop Shop,*
*Castle Farm, Shoreham, Sevenoaks, Kent TN14 7UB.*
*Telephone: (01959) 523219*

HERB PLANTS BY MAIL ORDER
*Jekka's Herb Farm,*
*Rose Cottage, Shellards Lane, Alveston, Bristol BS12 2SY.*
*Telephone: (01454) 418878*

HERB SEEDS
*Suffolk Seeds,*
*Monks Farm, Pantlings Lane, Coggeshall Road,*
*Kelvedon, Essex CO5 9PG.*
*Telephone: (01376) 572456*

PICTURE CREDITS
*Andrew Lawson Photography; p.14*